Change Your Frame
Then
Frame Your Change

Pastor Janice Graham-Randolph

Go Girlfriend Shine for Jesus Inc.

Flint, Michigan

Change Your Frame Then Frame Your Change
©2018 by Pastor Janice Graham-Randolph

All rights reserved. No part of this publication may be reproduced or transmitted in any form or by any means, electronic or mechanical, or any information storage or retrieval system, without prior permission of the author.

All Scriptures taken from Bible.Is a public domain Otherwise taken from:
Holy Bible Application® Copyrights @2008-2016
Used by Permission
SCSiriWaveformViewCopyright (c) 2013 Stefan Ceriu
Permission is hereby granted, free of charge, to any person obtaining a copy of this software and associated documentation files (the "Software"), to deal in the Software without restriction, including without limitation the rights to use, copy, modify, merge, publish, distribute, sublicense, and/or sell copies of the Software, and to permit persons to whom the Software is furnished to do so, subject to the following conditions: The above copyright notice and this permission notice shall be included in all copies or substantial portions of the Software.

All definitions take from the Cambridge Dictionary®
All Rights Reserved.

Published by Go Girlfriend Shine For Jesus Inc. Flint, Michigan 48532 Since 2019.

Cover Design by WWW.LAMAASH.BIZ

ISBN 978-0-578-491936

Printed in the United States
For Worldwide Distribution

Dedication

I would like to dedicate this book to my wonderful children and their spouses: Kenyata and Nakesia, Lasheca and Kareem Sr., and Calvin and Maria

To my wonderful grandchildren:
Kenyata Jr.,Ashanna, Ariel, Jania, Kareem Jr., Kameron, Satya, Calvin Santana, and Samir and great grandchildren: Paris and Payton the twins girls.

Acknowledgements

I would like to give appreciations to all those who have encouraged, coached, and mentored me through the years of my life:

Grandparents, Earl and Mint Graham who raised me from two months old

Biological parents, Alonzo Graham Sr. and Mary Hughes

Aunts and Uncles, Pastors, teachers, editors, and the Aspiring Writers Association of America, my coach in publishing, Cynthia Hatcher

Friends and family, especially my sister Kimberly and nephew Kaiden,
Craig and Maria, Linda, Jill, Janis and Curtis, Toy, Venita, Larry and Lisa, Inetta, Jane
My Employer, Dr. Elaine Gantz and Co-workers, Neighbors Steve and Marge
My community of Flint, Waterford, and Southfield, Michigan.

My home town Fort Meade, Florida, and my Los Angeles, California community
Comcast Cable TV, Stand, Step Up and Stretch Out for Jesus

Redeemed to Dominate Church of the Living God
Go Girlfriend Shine for Jesus Inc.

Pastor Larry A. and Carleen Holley.
Many thanks, blessings, and love to all of you.

To all those who read this book, may the Lord bless and keep you always and cause you to thrive to your highest God given potential.

Contents

Introduction

Chapter 1..........13
Time to Make a Change

Chapter 2..........19
Show and Tell

Chapter 3..........23
A Change has come Over Me

Chapter 4..........27
If God did it, if He said it, if He thought it, so can I!

Chapter 5..........31
Look Beyond Others Faults, Remember the Good Times

Chapter 6..........35
Give Honor to Whom Honor is Due, Best Dad in the Whole Wide World

Chapter 7..........39
Where There is a Will There is a Way

Chapter 8..........43
Time to Change My Frame

Chapter 9..........45
We Are Well Able! We Can Do It!

Chapter 10..........61
God's Perfect Frame for our Imperfect Frame

Chapter 11..........65
It's Time to Rise

Chapter 12..........69
A Better Plan

Chapter 13..........75
Think Like God (Have the Mind of Christ)

Chapter 14..........77
Recognize the Call of Greatness on Your Life

Chapter 15..........79
Creativity Begins

Chapter 16..........83
Revelation for Your Transformation

Chapter 17..........87
Faith in God Never Fails

Chapter 18..........93
Don't Play Around, Watch as Well as Pray

Change Your Frame

Then

Frame Your Change

Introduction

This revelation hit me so tough until I had to frame it in my mind and heart so no one or anything could break my frame of mind. To do what God does, to say what God says and to think like God thinks. It requires His wisdom, knowledge and understanding. I knew I wanted and needed it. I couldn't live without it. I hope you feel the same way after reading this book. It will change your life.

So travel along this journey with me. Watch God change your frame of shattered dreams, broken hearts, depression, intimidation, discouragements, victims of domestic violence, sadness, or whatever you are faced with. He will change the frame of mind set that's holding you back from being who you were created to be. He will tell you to take that frame of unforgiveness, to break that picture frame and throw it away, to put it behind you. It's history! Take another picture using His frame for your life, His magnificent Holy

Spirit, His Word, and I guarantee you won't ever want to take it off your wall. The frames on the walls of your heart, mind, and soul will now hold and show memories of peace, joy, love, and power to overcome any circumstance. He did it for me and He'll do it for you!

Chapter 1
Time to Make a Change

Let's look at what the word frame means.

1. A border that supports and surrounds a picture, door, or window.
2. The basic structure of a building, vehicle, or piece of furniture that other parts are added onto.
3. The size or shape of someone's body
4. Frame of mind- the way someone thinks or feels about something at a particular time.
5. Frame of reference- a set of ideas or facts accepted by a person that explains their behavior, opinions, or decisions.
6. Frame- game- a period of play in some games.

For some people change can be very difficult. To me change is another challenge and opportunity for me to grow and grow up. It can be uncomfortable but the results are gratifying. It's called becoming successful. You will find as you read this book all six definitions here will be utilized in some form to change the frame or picture of the way you've looked at yourself in the following areas: spiritually, physically, mentally, socially, and economically. It will also examine how you think and behave. The result will be how it's going to frame your life into one of the most beautiful portraits ever. You will never want to remove it from your wall. This frame is priceless.

Framing your change must begin with knowing about the Creator who has framed everything and everyone in His likeness and image. It also begins with knowing how He wanted this magnificent world and you to be that we live in.

He is an invisible God. He is Spirit but He changed the frame for everything to become visible. Let's use this analogy. Everything begins with an originator and then the invention is developed. This example is called a camera. A picture didn't just appear without a process and something to bring it to pass or something that is going to enhance and bring forth visibility and clarity. Once that picture or photograph is taken, it must go through a process using solutions for development such as developer and fixer solutions, rinsing off all residue with water. Now we can see it for what it is. A finalized picture that is able to be framed, ready to be shown to whosoever it's presented to. It can't be changed from the original state.

If we recall the frame of mind this world was in before God breathed on it, it was void, empty and chaotic. It was in a state of confusion and disorder. It was like a lot of lives and this world today. He had to show us the way to transform our lives from chaotic darkness to a state of peace and light. To a new way of living and that was only through Jesus Christ.

He had inspired men of God write of the mess this world was in, but He showed us the way of escape from the ball of confusion. We were so deceived by the devil back in the day because of the lack of

God's knowledge. A song written by the Temptations many years ago was title *Ball of Confusion*. It is still prevalent today. This writer wrote what he saw and probably what he experienced. His frame was full of a mass of confusion and disruption in our world. It has come to pass again.

With the help of the Holy Spirit, I want to help us change our frame then frame our change into the most beautiful image God will be pleased with. I want this frame to be a shield, a barrier, a protector from the chaos in the world. We are in this world but not of it. We are partakers of an inheritance we can be assured of.

Many years ago, Marvin Gaye sang a song titled, *What's Going On*. People write how they feel to release the pressure of life. The songs of this world are temporal. This may be due to the fact this is what's going on. The frame, the picture, is visible. It's even what's going on, but is it the truth. Jesus says "My Word is Truth and Life."

We can ponder on this question... is the way of the world supposed to be the lifestyle of the people of God? Our lives should have a different path. There is a scripture in the Bible that I read which says to *call those things that be not as though they were.* In other words, call whatever we want to come to pass in our lives. We should call it out, sing it out, speak it out, or preach it out. We do this if we want to see it come to pass! We must change what we say, then we will change what we see. We can't talk about the way we are, we talk about what we want to be. We are snared by the words of our mouths. We must start making positive declarations over our lives, the lives of our children, and our environment according to the will and Word of God. We have framed and caused so many negative issues, circumstances, and problems to come to pass in our lives. We do this because of one little member in this body...the tongue. Some things are passed down from our generations that are negative and generational curses. Jesus Christ came to deliver from the curse of the law of sin, sickness, poverty, and death. Isn't that amazing!

Chapter 2
Show and Tell

Show and Tell was a beautiful, positive love song sang by Al Wilson years ago. He was speaking in relation to a man who had such a powerful love for his woman. It reminded me of a mother who had a love for God so much that she would do anything for Him. Her Frame was so sure and steadfast. The magnitude of her love for God the Father goes beyond the love for her fiancé, Joseph. This was not a game she played though, she was sincere. She was not afraid to accept the challenge, the ridicule, rejection of her future husband, and the accusations. She also endured the pain of her son when he was crucified on the cross for doing good. I'm sure with all she had to face, that frame was something to behold. She had to change her frame of the negative images that was put before her and start creating her new frame. This one was far better than the one she left behind. Imagine being divorced from someone before you even get married. What a frame to change. But she did. I doubt it crossed her mind giving up this new frame of eternal wisdom, destiny, hope, peace, life and grace. She left that frame of discouragement and didn't look back. Her faith to press on caused the angel of the Lord to come down to fight for her God given destiny with her husband Joseph and cousin Elizabeth. Thank God He interceded in that relationship, spoke to that man and put some sense in his head. We already had Eve listening to devil's voice of deception, we didn't need another decade of trouble from Joseph.

She had the Savior of the world on the inside of her, Jehovah Jireh the everlasting provider, and Jehovah Rafa her healer. She didn't ever have to be sick again. Inside of her was Jehovah Nissi, her refuge and protector. No one could ever harm her. She didn't let anyone or anything stop her. She kept it moving and went to help and encourage her cousin Elizabeth to bring forth and birth her destiny, John the

Baptist. Those two sisters knew how to get breakthroughs.

With all that power on the inside of them, God had to shut Zachariah's mouth. That one little member, is powerful, our tongue can heal or destroy.

Be it unto me according to (agreeing with) your word Lord.(Luke 1:38)This is one of my favorite scriptures and one of the most qualified, eligible, faithful, believers of all times, the mother of our Lord Jesus Christ. She changed her frame then she framed her change by allowing God's word to be it unto her according to His word. In doing so, she became the mother of our Lord and Savior Jesus Christ. Out of her mouth what she spoke was positive blessings. She believed and had faith saying, "For with God all things are possible." (Luke 1:37)

She showed and told! She spoke it! She believed it! She received it and God did it!

Chapter 3
A Change has Come Over Me

There was a man named Jabez. He changed his frame then framed his change to the type of frame God created him to have for his life. This man had to live with a name his mother gave him because of her pain and the mishaps in her life. What a way to set a future for a child. I can imagine when he grew up and found out the significant meaning of his name, he wanted to know why his mother would name him that…Pain. This young man still remained honorable not allowing the negativity that was passed down to him due to something that was out of his control. Instead he put his faith to work. Names meant something in biblical days. It put a course to your destiny.

Now Jabez knew he had to do something about his future and it started with the changing of his frame, not his name. This was deeper. It was an image he had been looking at for years, reflections of broken dreams of poverty and lack, memories of causing his mother so much pain birthing him. He had to show his mother and others that this frame was about to change.

He went to the Originator of his life. He needed the One who had begun the work in him to complete it. He dealt with the Author and Finisher of his faith. He had a name, a frame, a plan, for him before the foundation of the world. He knew the plan was a good plan, a plan not for evil or calamity and sorrow. He had read about how his forefathers had been blessed by Him. He fought for them, giving victory after victory and there was no respecter of persons. He believed if He did it for them, he knew He would do it for him.

I'm sure he said to himself "I am redeemed and blessed. There is increase, protection, provision, preservation, and favor for me. I know now that the blessing of the Lord maketh rich and addeth no sorrow or pain with it! I don't have to live with the shame any longer. Mom, thank you for going through the pain for me. Now the one who caused you so much pain is going to show you how you can change your pain into gain because nothing is too hard or impossible for my God!

I can just imagine in my mind how Jabez was feeling at this time. He changed his frame from a frame of shame, defeat and ridicule to a frame of victory, blessing and favor, peace and prosperity! He believed if he asked God to do it He would and He did.

> *And Jabez was more honorable than his brethren: and his mother called his name Jabez, saying, because I bare him with sorrow. And Jabez called on the God of Israel, saying, Oh that thou wouldest bless me indeed, and enlarge my territories/coast, and that thine hand might be with me, and that thou wouldest keep me from evil, that it might not grieve me(cause me sorrow/pain) And God granted him that which he requested.*
> (1 Chronicles 4:9-10)

He spoke it! He believed it! He received it! God did it!

Chapter 4
If God Did It, If He Said It, If He Thought It, So Can I!

How do you see yourself? I challenge you to see yourself as God sees you. You are fearfully and wonderfully made. Framed!

What happens when you are thrown into a life and lifestyle that's out of your hands and out of your control? Moses, Joseph, Esther, Jabez, and so many other people in God's Word were chosen by God and had a call of greatness on their lives. They weren't perfect and had some serious issues going on. But to God, He sees you in your future frame, fearfully and wonderfully made...framed. We start out as this beautiful angel of our parents. They don't ever want to leave you or put you down. Then as years pass by and challenges come not just one day but years of dealing with all kinds of frustrations, dilemmas, and dramas. The way we see our child then becomes, "What happened to you? You've changed into another person."

We get older, less patient and we wonder, Lord is this really my child? Did they make a mistake and give me the wrong one? When we realize, yes this child is mine, we can't deny we are a frame of their past. Some pictures are so beautiful while others are hurtful reminders. Go back and remember the great times like when you brought them home, held them in your arms and kissed them over and over again. Watch your spirit rise to another level of hope. My grandparents always thought I was their angel, their baby, even when I know I broke their hearts time and time again. Not intentionally but ignorantly. They would remind me of when they went to get me how I was so beautiful and I was theirs no matter what.

Change is not comfortable sometimes. I felt like Mosetta and Josetta (Moses and Joseph) at times in my life after I had grown up and start experiencing hard times. Over time I learned, you take the lemon life and make lemonade out of it. You make the bitter, sweet. We used to have a tree in the back of our home that was called a Bitter

Sweet tree. It would bare bitter sweet fruit. It looked like a bumpy, ugly orange. The taste was in-between an orange and lemon. It would make the best sweet juice ever. We would squeeze the fruits, add water and sugar. It was good. When life starts squeezing, pressuring, and pushing your back against the wall, this is what you have to do with life. Take the bitter with the sweet. Turn it into the best fruit juice ever. Start rejoicing and giving praise to Jesus and watch your pains and pressures turn to power, potential, and peace that surpasses all your understanding.

I realized I was redeemed to dominate my issues, not to allow my issues to dominate me. Live your life to the fullest taking dominion over every evil work of the devil. Don't remain bitter and sweet. Get better and sweeter, a little lesson from my Bitter Sweet tree.

Chapter 5
Look Beyond Others Faults, Remember the Good Times

Daddy Boot- T. That's what they called him. His name was Alonzo. He wore his hat, boots, and dress so dignified, clean cut, just like a Texan cattle man. He could wheel and deal with bankers in our town and get money to do whatever he wanted. People couldn't understand how he could do what they couldn't. It's called the favor of God. I didn't know that back then.

"God bless the child that's got his own Janice," that's what my dad would always tell me when I would come to his home to visit. We'd talk and talk and all of sudden he would start talking about Jesus. He would then burst out with one of his favorite scriptures and say, "Eyes hath not seen nor ear heard what God has in store (has plan) for those who love him and those who are called according to His purpose." He would always say God had been so merciful to him and he had not been the greatest father or husband. But he would thank God for another chance to change his life and to appreciate the people in his life.

My dad was a strong willed man and didn't back down for no one. He was a farmer and a cattleman. He served in the military as well. When he came out he bought up land and planted vegetables and the family worked those fields. He bought his own cattle, raised them and sold them. He went and bought one of the biggest properties in our home town and built one of the biggest homes there. He put his cattle all around it and everyone in town, just like his parents, my grandparents, Earl and Mint, knew how to invest and make a difference so that his family would never be without. Some of us grasped hold to the vision and some didn't. My biological dad was a man who had vision like Abraham in the Bible. Not only that, it was like my Heavenly Father. He had the cattle of many. Seemed like to me, all around his land, he would call each one by their name and they would come running. He was amazing in his own way even though he didn't raise me. I learned so much from him by just observing his business strategy. He worked diligently to make things happened that seemed impossible. He had cattle on other lands he had purchased.

I took my eyes off of the mistakes my parents made in life and started focusing on the overwhelming victories and the grace and mercies of God on their lives. When I did that, my life changed drastically. Love truly covers a multitude of sins. My dad changed his frame then framed his change.

Chapter 6
Give Honor to Whom Honor is Due
Best Dad in the Whole World

Daddy Earl. That's what my family called him. He was Daddy to me. My grandfather and dad could quote scriptures like crazy. I would love to sit and listen to them talk about the goodness of the Lord then they would listen to me and we would have such a wonderful time together. I would sit by my grandfather while he was in that rocking chair and I was on a little stool. It was like a little girl sitting on her father's lap with her arms around his neck just enjoying being together. Even when I was grown and gone, when I came home I would sit on his lap and give him a big hug. Then I would rub his knees for him because he said they would hurt.

I was the only one he would let touch his knees. He would let me know they felt much better after I rubbed them. That man could build anything. He had a six grade education and his mind was as sharp and brilliant as a genius. I know that God was with him and gave him knowledge on how to build and hook up any electrical device. He built all my dressers and my own bed. The heavy, thick wood, he varnished and painted it so beautiful. He built our home, the cabinets in the kitchen and his own little room where he had a bed when he wanted to get away. I loved this room because it was the music studio where daddy had all kinds of music. He loved gospel, quartet music, and jazz. He knew I loved music and loved to sing and dance. So he wired and hooked a system from his music studio to the house. Every room had a speaker in it to listen to music whenever we wanted. My grandfather was gifted and talented.

He was a Deacon at the church too but somehow along his journey he stop going. God has a way of drawing that is so amazing. Just out of the blue Daddy just started going back to church. Each Sunday morning he would go to the members' home to collect their offerings if they were unable to come to church. He just started serving. It was so good to see him over in that corner and my grandmother ushering each Sunday.

Dad worked at what they called a phosphate mine as well. He and my grandmother could sing too. There were things people had to do back then to survive that was legal for the whites because they were the ones approved for licenses to do these things.

My daddy changed his frame then framed his change.

Chapter 7
Where There is a Will There is a Way

Mom Mint. That's what they called her but she was Momma to me. Down south, our people, figured out a way to survive around the politics and prejudice. Where there's a will, there's a way. Everything that was legal for them to prosper was illegal for us.

I remember when they came to the house and took my grandmother to jail for selling numbers or what they called back then Boletta. What we call Motels, they called Rooming Houses. They were entrepreneurs. Back then, seasonal workers would need a room to rest and stay for the orange picking season. My grandparents knew how to make money come to them. Black people were labeled as not knowledgeable and always having to work the fields for a living. They would get robbed and cheated of their rightful earnings. But my grandparents had another plan for their lives.

I thought it was just a bingo game. I was young then. It looked to be so much fun. They would spin the balls and draw three numbers and whatever numbers were chosen that night would be the winning number. And people would win big money for being the winner. Someone of our own who was jealous because my grandparents were wealthy and had gained a lot of respect in that little town, turned my grandmother in. That was the saddest day of my life. I saw them take her away from me. I cried and cried. Police were everywhere. You would have thought she murdered someone. To me it was just a game they were playing making money. But to the white people, it was illegal. Blacks had figured out a way to prosper and they couldn't get a piece of the pie.

Now it is the biggest money maker in the world. It's called the lottery and bingo. Before it was called the Number Racket and Boletta. My grandmother went through all of that hardship and now it's legal.

Isn't that something how people can steal your ideas that you suffered for, take it and run with it? Give it to the biggest crooks in town just because they got the money to make it happen. But thanks be to God they couldn't keep my grandmother in that jail long. My grandfather got her out that jail so quick you would have thought he was the road runner. He had the Lord on his side and money that they didn't know he had. He got his wife out.

My grandmother and granddaddy had some shonuff favor with God and man. After that, white folk and black folk knew don't mess with the Graham family. He loved that woman and would do anything for her. He went and bought my Momma the biggest, newest, prettiest Cadillac in Fort Meade. It was pearly white and gold. She always took immaculate care of that man. He never went lacking of nothing. He knew he was gonna be taken care of. I was the happiest child in the world to see my Momma back home.

Years later I found out this was called gambling. But I couldn't judge. People did what they had to do to survive and they were having fun doing it. Churches and other organizations playing numbers and Boletta it's not gambling now, it just a game used for winning prizes and money. It is supposed to help the schools but here in Michigan more schools are closed down. I wonder where all the money is going.

My grandparents were difference makers. They raised me from two months old. They were world changers. They knew how to change their frame then frame their change. They made their own businesses and I see that what they started, now people all over the world is rich and famous. Just different names and frames changed.

Chapter 8
Time to Change My Frame

I started observing the life of myself and the lives of others including the life of my biological Dad and my Mom Mary.

You will get out of life what you put into it. Janice Life 101. Some people never changed their old frame. They keep up the same picture. It's the same images of themselves, same lifestyles, environment, talk the same old filthy way, cursing and fussing, and fighting. It's their lifestyle, shacking then packing, never stable. Lifestyle of adulterers and fornicating is their mind set. "I'm okay just the way I am," they say. We didn't realize the devil was our god.

People do own a lot of things as you can see. They possessed and owned all these frames of future heartbreak and headaches, unhappiness then death, they are living to die instead of dying to live. We should be loving to live then living to love. God does rain on the just and the unjust but is that rain gonna water good seed or bad weed?

Whatever we plant in life will come up if we don't change the frame of our minds. We must change the frame of our words, change the frame of our vision and change the frame of how we do things. If we keep doing the same things over and over again getting the same results then our frame will remain the same. If we want to change the frame of our bodies due to overeating and lack of exercise, we have to put a plan of action in motion. Then our frame will change when we frame the change of the pattern of our mindsets, eating habits and exercising regularly.

I had to do all of the above and God has truly blessed me and my seed indeed.

Chapter 9
We Are Well Able! We Can Do it!

<u>Prime Examples the Shaping of My Life</u>
<u>Go For the Milk and Honey</u>

I had to change my focus and my view. My mindset had to change from how I used to think to how my new Master thinks.

In the heat of the moment all of us have spoken words we wished we had never said. These are words we can't take back. There are ways to rectify what was spoken wrongly, to put something right, or make things right. Joshua and Caleb can help us.

Joshua and Caleb spoke only positive words. They change their frame from all the negativity and evil that surrounded them and trusted God's word. God commanded Moses to instruct the spies to go up into the mountain, search the land out for it was a land that floweth with milk and honey. (Numbers 13-14)

> ...and see the land, what it is; and the people that dwell in it, whether they be

strong or weak, few or many, and what the land they dwell in whether it be good or bad, and what cities they be that they dwell in, whether in tents or strong holds, and what the land is whether it be fat (prosperous) or lean(lacking); whether it be wood in it or not, then He said be of good courage, and bring of the fruit of the land.
(Numbers 13:18-20)

Caleb and Joshua saw the same giants, large giants, tall buildings, and humongous fruit, but the bible said they had a different spirit. The spirit that was within them was greater than the spirit that surrounded them. This is how they conquered and defeated the oppositions of the evil reports of their brethren they were faced with. They came back with a good report.

Caleb stilled all the people and said, let us go up at once, and possess it; for we be well able to overcome it.
(Numbers 13:30)

Doubt, unbelief, and fears destroy your dreams and destiny. The negative report, the Bible calls it an evil report, was brought back by the ten spies who were so scared they withstood Caleb in front of everybody saying, *"we are not able to go up against this people they are stronger than we are"* (Numbers 13:31). The Bible said they brought up an evil report. They told everyone,"the land was a land that eateth up the inhabitants, and all the people they saw in it was of great stature. We saw the giants and we were in our own sight as grasshoppers." (Numbers 13:22)

Their report was so convincing they stirred up all the congregation until all the people cried and they wept all that night. The next day they murmured against Moses and Aaron and wished they stayed in Egypt. What a sad bunch of people. They liked being slaves, beating and eating leftovers. How low-minded and scared can one be? That's what fear does to you. It causes you to doubt and give up on ones who have stuck with you through the thick and thin.

Then Joshua and Caleb tried to calm this mob down but they turned on them and tried to stone them. But God intervened. His Glory appeared to the whole congregation. God was very angry, so angry He was about to wipe them all out except the ones who believed. Moses, the man of God, interceded for them so tough until God changed His mind with His judgment of the death sentence. He pardoned them according to the word of Moses. He said there would still be a consequence. Those who were twenty years and up would wander in the wilderness for forty years. This was just because of the evil report they brought back that caused a generation of people to fear and doubt the Word of God to be plagued and destroyed.

The evil reporters feared the giants, the fear of growing up and facing the fear of people. They feared the humongous fruit, the fear of having to change their attitudes, fear of dealing with those who may have more in life than they did, and the ones who accomplished more. They feared large buildings. They feared growth, character changes, increase multiplication, advancing, and change of how we used to live. They feared changing into a new environment, the fears of being captured, then the fear of losing the battle, and the fear of defeat.

The fight in us seems to weaken under pressure, challenge, difference and change. The brethren had brought back a bad report of the land that God had told them was theirs. They were challenged and surrounded with doubts and fears that took over their minds. Then was spoken out of their mouths and this was the defeat.

> *Out of the abundance of the heart the mouth speaketh. A good man out of the treasure of his heart bringeth forth good things: and an evil man out of evil treasure bringeth forth evil things. For by thy words you shall be justified, and by your words you shall be condemned.*
> (Matthew 12: 34b-35, 37)

The others spoke words of doubt and unbelief condemned them. They didn't change their frame.

Joshua and Caleb's victory is ours too! They had to frame their change with a good report, a vision of we are well able and we can do it. We can go in and possess the land. God blessed and rewarded them. The majority doesn't always win. Their faith and belief in what God promised gave them victory over the doubtful, fearful evil reports of the other ten spies. Their frame said we are well able to go and possess the land. Their frame didn't show doubt and fear. We can take dominion over every challenge we face. Whether sickness and disease, poverty and lack, bad attitudes, negativity, doubts and fears all can be changed and delivered if we only believe.

They showed we can do all things through Christ which strengthens us.
(Philippians 4:13)They changed their frame then framed their change.

Moses- He Changed His Frame
A Call of Greatness

Moses was a man put in a position that was out of his control. His mother had to give her child away due to a decree ordered by the Pharaoh of that day. The decree stated for all first born male children to be killed. But God had a call of greatness on his life that not even powerful men in authority could stop. This is how I had to start believing that no matter what happened to me, whether good or bad, the call of greatness on my life can't be stopped by no man or woman. All things are going to work out for my good because I'm called according to His purpose.

Moses was a man who went from, "I can't do this, I can't speak well but I can with God. If you give me something to work with Lord I can."

God said, "What do you have in your hand?"

He said, "A Rod."

God said, "Then stretch it out!"

And the rest is history. What do you have in your hand? Use it before you lose it.

Moses' change was by allowing God to work with his speech impediment, his temper, fears and his doubts. Then he framed his change into becoming one of the meekest men of God. He was the bravest deliverer of God's people Israel ever had, delivering them from a mindset of slavery to an ownership mentality. He assisted in turning their hearts from worshiping idols to worshiping the Most High God, Jehovah Jireh their provider.

The Samaritan Woman at the Well

Jesus just has a way of drawing like no other. This fantastic woman changed her frame by totally surrendering her life to Jesus. She carried around these frames of adultery, shacking, some say divorced five times, but to me it could have been five husbands of other women. It clearly states by her when Jesus tells her to go bring back her husband if she wants this living water, she says she had no husband and Jesus brings it on home by saying you're right! You don't have a husband, for you have had five husbands. He didn't say the five husbands she had were her husbands. He told her later the one you now live with is not your husband. She perceived that Jesus was a prophet and her whole life changed. The Messiah was communing with her, the Savior of the world! She dropped her waterpot, her old frame of lifestyle, all her excess garbage. She dropped that man she was in bondage with and all the other men she left behind. She went and told all the other men of the city about a man who told her about all her business and everything she had ever done and who she done it with. What a frame or image to be looking at every day. Her life was no longer that name of shame and a frame of shame. She no longer allowed others to intimidate her life or control it. This remarkable deliverance at the well became a well of new life. This was a changed life, springing out of her, who caused a whole city, especially the men who had encounters with her in relationships. She changed her frame then framed her change a new way of living, the abundant life.

I can really relate to this woman because I was a runaway child running wild. That song by the Temptations, *Runaway Child* was me. The devil had me out there wild and crazy living a promiscuous lifestyle because I had left my first love...Jesus Christ. When God says He chastise those He loves, I believed the Lord loved me a whole lot. The whippings were nothing like Grandmother's and Granddad's. I thought they were hard. I could really appreciate them then more than ever. Shacking with my boyfriend, didn't want to get married just wanted to get out the house of my uncle and aunt. This was all because a young man was telling me how much he loved me and he would take good care of me. They were all just a pack of lies and deception. But I was out there. I just couldn't go back home where I belonged because I was in Los Angeles, California. I was a long way from Florida. I could go but was ashamed and afraid.

My life was in such a shamble running away from men who was threatening to kill me. Thank God I didn't get into heavy drugs or anything like that but was turned on to marijuana. I thought I was losing it! I started hallucinating and thought somebody was trying to kill me. This stuff was not for me.

Sex was not fulfilling either. I just did it because my boyfriend wanted it, sad but true. I learned how to fake it very well. I just wanted it over. I didn't even have a lot of male companions I can count on one hand, see how I can relate to this woman. I wasn't married to them and that's what made it wrong and that's where my chastisement came in. I experienced abuse terribly. I wasn't a heavy drinker but one night I went to a club and I decided to have what they called a Bloody Mary. I thought because the drink had tomato juice in it that it was healthy. That night the sharp pains began to hit me one after another. They took me to emergency and took me to surgery right away. A cyst had burst inside. Just like the marijuana, never will I take a drink of any kind again. The devil was trying his best to kill me but God always was watching over me giving me warning after warning.

I tried shacking again. That was the wrong move. Again it was abuse, distrust, and fighting. I had my first son before I got married and it changed my whole life. My frame really had to change because Doctors said I couldn't have children but they don't know everything. He's my first miracle.

I finally got married and had a miscarriage but God came through again. I had two more miracle children. Miracles just kept happening in my life. Even though the marriage was rocky, it lasted for thirty years. Once within that thirty years, we almost divorced. We decided to try and make it work. Later on we just couldn't make it work. This was a hard trial for me. Being a pastor's wife, I never thought I would be getting a divorce. The shame, along with people talking without knowing what happened. It was a hard decision I had to face and God helped me through it. Now I am so happy. I never thought I would get my life back. God can bless you so good when you forget all the wrong people had done to you. Like Joseph said God caused me to forget all the wrong my brethren had done to me. Thanks be to God I came to myself like the prodigal son and realized how well I have it at home with my Father. Now I can run and tell everybody about the great things God has done for me. No more shame in my frame.

Mary, The Woman with Seven Demons
She Changed Her Frame Then Framed Her Change

Imagine not being able to live in a society scandalized, criticized, ostracized called crazy, out of your mind every day, and nobody wanting to be around you. I can imagine her life being a living hell! This was her before pictured life. Her frame of evil, demonic oppression and depression was out of her control.

In biblical days, people would pay false prophets of the devil or Baal/ Beelzebub/ to put curses on people lives and their families. The name Baal is drawn from the Canaanite deity mentioned in the Hebrew Bible. He was one of the seven princes of hell. He is mentioned widely in the Old Testament as the primary pagan idol of the Phoenicians often associated with the heathen goddess Ashtaroth also meaning lord not Lord.

People did not know how to reverse the curses off of their lives. But along came Jesus to set at liberty the captives, to heal the broken hearted, the battered and bruised, and open the blinded eyes. This woman fell at Jesus' feet. She bowed down and washed his feet with her tears and hair and could care less who was saying or thinking anything of how she was caring for the Master. At that time satan had no more power or control over her life. Jesus became her Lord and Master. She was free from tortured demonic spirits who tormented her day and night and the agonizing pain. Her worship was to her Creator of heaven and earth and satan could no longer touch her. Every demon had to flee!

Your praise and worship stills the enemy. When you submit yourself to God, resist the devil, the enemy has to flee. This is how we have to be when it comes to worship, no shame. He's our Lord and we will have no other gods before Him. Be willing to change your frame of that old life then frame your change of your new life knowing and believing all things are possible to those who believe. She never looked back or went back. Would You?

Therefore if any man be in Christ he is a new creation: (creature) behold old things are passed away; behold all things are become new.
(2 Corinthians 5:17)

Chapter 10
God's Perfect Frame for Our Imperfect Frame

This perfect frame is just waiting on you and I. He had to reform, refashion, recreate, and reframe this world for us to live in it. It wasn't a pretty picture. God had a picture in his mind already of how he wanted this world to be You and I are a part of that perfect picture. His choice of words, were good and very good. Be ye perfect as He is perfect. The Psalmist 139:15 says "My frame was not hidden from thee, when I was made in secret, and curiously wrought in the lowest parts of the earth." ASV

Thine eyes did see mine unformed substance; and in thy book they were all written, even the days that were ordained for me
(Psalms 139:16ASV)

Everybody has different frames but you can believe He knows yours. He created a perfect world which consisted of good and also evil, for a purpose of maintaining peace, love, harmony, discipline, and by whatever means necessary. He did not create this magnificent world without having a plan for correction.

All scripture (His Word) is given by inspiration of God and is profitable for doctrine, for reproof, for correction, for instruction in righteousness: that the man or woman of God may be perfect thoroughly furnished unto all good works.
(2 Timothy 3:16, 17)

There is a plan for protection, provision and order for His creation.

My God shall supply all my need according to his riches in glory by Christ Jesus.
(Philippians 4:19)

God is not going to create anyone or anything greater or more powerful than Him, it wouldn't make sense. Atheism is beyond a fool. A fool says in their heart there is no God. Atheism goes beyond believing there is no God. They say that no one created anything. It just appeared out of nowhere. In reality they don't want to give any credit to anybody. They don't want to recognize there is a God that they can't see or feel so they choose to denounce there is no one responsible for them being created. Why? There will be no one to blame for his or her actions also there is absence of belief. No need for restraints. It is, was it is, according to atheism. Now some Christians are saying the same thing.

The only thing that is what it is, is the Word of God. It is what it is!

Chapter 11
It's Time to Rise

Everything God spoke was good. How much more does He want good things to come forth out of our mouths? If we as a people can get this we could change the frame of our lives and the lives of so many people in this dying world.

Look what God says to us: Psalms 34:11-14

Come, ye children, hearken unto me, I will teach you the fear of the Lord.

He asked a question.

What man/ person is he that desireth life, and loveth many days, that he may see good?

Then He answered the question because He knows nobody in their right mind would not want to live and experience a good long life. He says keep your tongue from evil, and your lips from speaking guile(lies and deceit).

Depart from evil, and do good; seek peace and pursue it.

How did God do it? How did He frame, fashion, create, form His frame from one destiny to another?

> *...through faith we understand that the worlds or kingdoms were framed by the word of God, so that things which are seen were not made of things which do appear (or so that what is seen was not made or created or framed out of what was visible. by human ability.)*
> (Hebrews 11:3)

It is going to take faith, believing, having confidence, and having assurance in His Word that we are going to do what He did.

All these patriots' frame had to change at one time or another, a picture of faults and failures. Look at them now. That frame they have is written and framed in the Perfect Hall of Faith the Everlasting Frame of our Lord and Savior Jesus Christ. What a portrait to be a part of, framed and sealed forever.

These were all commended (applauded) for their faith (had a good reputation), (yet none of them received all that God had promised them)since God had planned something better for us in mind, so that only together with us would they be made perfect.
(Hebrews 11:39-40)

This is what we must always remember God always have a better plan for our lives than we do.

Chapter 12
A Better Plan

Isn't it amazing how God spoke into existent something that was once nothing then spoke into existent what He wanted to come to pass. He called it the heavens and the earth. The earth was the ground, the dirt in which He formed and created man out of. He used it for vegetation and growth for means of survival and nurture.

He used something that in the natural would seemed insignificant and of no value, to create the most important and valuable creature that exist on this human planet. Other than His Son, we are just a little lower than the angels.

What is man that thou are mindful of him? and the son of man that thou visiteth him? For thou has made him a little lower than the angels, and hast crowned him with glory and honor. Thou madest him to have dominion over the works of thy hands; thou has put all things under his feet.
(Psalms 8:4-6)

Deut. 30:9 says God will make you plenteous in every work of your hand, in the fruit of your body, in the fruit of your cattle, and the fruit of your land, for good: as he rejoiced over your fathers.

This is contingent upon us hearkening unto the voice of the Lord thy God (your God), to keep His commandments and His statues which are written in this book of the law, and if thou (you) turn unto the Lord thy God with all thy heart, and with all thy (your) soul.

This is a part of how we rise to the top.

> *And the Lord God formed (framed) man of the dust of the ground, and breathed into his nostrils the breath of life; (he used his mouth) and man became a living soul. (Man was framed into a living soul.)*
> (Genesis 2:7)

This reminds me of how the potter takes the clay, gathers it all together, forms or frames his vessel to how he pictures or imagines in his mind what he wants it to look like. He doesn't stop until he has perfected it exactly as he desires.

God could have just framed man as a statue of clay, of liberty, or of stone, but it wouldn't have been like Him. He knows without His breath of life breathed in to a statue of dirt or statue of clay, our souls would have been dead and lost.

1Peter 2:5 says we are now lively stones, are build up a spiritual house, an holy priesthood, to offer up spiritual sacrifices, acceptable to God by Jesus Christ. He would not have been able to communicate and have a relationship with dead dry stones and bones. (Ezekiel 37:3)

God asked Ezekiel a question, "Can these (dry) bones live?"

He answered, "Sovereign Lord, You alone know."

Again He said to me; prophesy over these bones and say to them, oh dry bones, hear the word of the Lord Thus says the Lord God unto these bones; Behold I will cause breath to enter into you, and you shall live.
(Ezekiel 37:3)

In order for us to rise in life we are going to have to do what God, our Heavenly Father did...start thinking and start speaking! God spoke into existence what He wanted it to be with His mouth.

He did something so powerful before He spoke. To begin anything you must have an imagination of a thing, person, place or destiny. God created this world by imagining, fashioning, forming, framing, and creating how He wanted it in His mind. He thought, hey this is what I want done first this is how I want it to begin.

In the beginning God created (framed, formed) the heaven and the earth.
(Genesis 1:1)

He had to let man know He is the creator, originator, framer, fashioner, of what you are about to witness. In my mind, God says I've planned, imagined, and framed, this. This is what I want my heaven and earth to be.

There is a movie titled, *Think Like a Man*. I beg to differ that is so far from the truth let me inform you to change the way you think.

Think like God. Change what you speak, what you believe, and how you live. You will frame the most beautiful portrait to remember for eternity. Change your frame then frame your change. You will never be the same.

Chapter 13
Think Like God

Proverbs 23:7 says as a man thinketh, in his heart so is he.

We should have the mind of Christ. This is why it's so important that we don't allow our minds to feast on things that are not good for us. Our minds become void of His understanding, contaminated, intoxicated, depressed and chaotic. This is what happens when you think like the world.

Jeremiah had a call on his life to save God's people. Before he was formed or framed in his mother's womb, God sanctified him, and ordained him, to pluck up, to breakdown, to destroy and to overthrow, to build and to plant. They called him the Weeping Prophet because of the calling on his life. He was to save the people of God and to deliver them. He would weep because they would not listen to the word of deliverance. He had to change his frame of thinking that he was not capable of the task because he was too young. God had to build him up in his thinking letting him know when I am with you nothing is impossible. That frame of fear and impossibility became a frame of possibility.

Life must have been overwhelming for Jeremiah when he was very young. No time for video games, sports activities, or playing with his friends. His childhood was snatched away because God predestined his life for His purpose. I'm so glad that we have a God that we can talk to even when we're young when we have insecurities and doubts. He will reassure us that everything will be alright if we just trust Him.

Sometimes all you see are the forks in the roads, the pitfalls, the clay instead of the beautiful vessel. The excuses are; this is too hard, I'm too young, I'm not ready to let my life go yet, people will talk about me, I'm too old, I don't have the finances, or I'm a woman. Isn't it amazing how God can see a call of greatness on your life before you can?

Chapter 14
Recognize the Call of Greatness on Your Life

People every day are walking around going through hardships because they can't figure out what they want to do in life. They keep suffering, listening to everybody suggestions telling them they are so good at this or that. You would be great and successful if you did this or that. Or they may tell you that you can't do this because it's not like you. They may say things like your mom or dad won't agree if you did this or your pastor or best friend say that's not you. Creative minds listen to their God given talents and work to perfect those gifts.

Those who are born again listen to the Spirit of God. I was born to sing and I'm very good at it, but that didn't pay my bills, put food on my table or pay my house note. There were people telling me to quit my job and start my own business or work for them. Now their businesses are all failing. They are struggling and everyone who follows them is struggling. I had to tune out the negativity and everybody's guidance for my life and start focusing on where the Lord was guiding me. I listened to God and have been very successful in what I do and that's dental assisting. I'm still singing and now writing. They told me I couldn't Pastor and evangelize because I was a woman but I'm doing it too and loving it. The Bible says I would be blessed in the city and blessed in the field. If I commit my way unto the Lord, He will establish my goings. Wherever God plants you and everyplace your feet shall tread upon, He has given it to you. You just have to wait on God, be of good courage and don't let people discourage what He has put on the inside of you. Recognizing the greatness in you will cause doors to open that you never dreamed of. When you listen to the Spirit of God, He will never lead you in the wrong direction.

Chapter 15
Creativity Begins

The definition of create is to originate, build, frame, fashion, shape, fabricate, mold.

The definition of form is to shape, mold, make, fashion, construct, design, produce, build, create, information blank, develop, contour, outline, frame, sculptured.

What type of atmosphere or life are you creating? Let's start with prayer.

Prayer is an essential element you must develop in your life. It creates the atmosphere of your environment. When I was a little girl my grandmother always, by example, showed me how to pray each night before I went to bed. I would always get on my knees and say the Lord's Prayer just like she did. I would always have such disturbing dreams but when I prayed, my sleep was peaceful. She would read her Bible at night before she went to bed. I saw this and it developed in me. But when I moved away from home, I started to neglect those teachings and my life became difficult, chaotic, scary, and lonely...until I remembered my upbringing. Life still has its' challenges but now I had a higher power, the Most High God with me helping me each day. What a relief!

Prayer is the key to the kingdom and your faith unlocks the door. (See Matthew 6:5-15)You have an adversary, the devil, Peter puts so plain.

1Peter 5:8 says be sober, (alert), be vigilant; because your adversary (enemy) the devil, walketh about as a roaring lion, seeking whom he may devour (destroy).

We have to watch as well as pray. Preparation and creativity goes hand and hand. You need them both to succeed. Start each day with prayer and meditation of the Word of God.

In Psalms 1:1-3 it is written to meditate day and night. In John 15:5 Jesus is speaking:"I am the true vine, you are the branches: he that abideth in me, and I in him, the same bringeth forth much fruit: for without me you can do nothing."

Chapter 16
Revelation for your Transformation

Genesis 1:2

So the earth had no unction to function. Nothing was in operation. No abilities for possibilities.

Void— (adj) useless, empty, barren, destitute, vacant, abandon, no frame, unoccupied, fruitless, without purpose.

(n) nothingness, emptiness, space, vacuum

> *The earth was a shapeless, chaotic mass, with the Spirit of God brooding over the dark vapors.*
> (Genesis 1:2)

It wasn't until God breathed His breath or anointing on the face of the deep that the resources of the earth could be useful and valuable for our benefit.

Recognize you are nothing and can be nothing without Him. Notice how and why I keep taking you back to the beginning. Your successful future starts when you know who your Creator is and believe if He started this work in you He will complete it.

In speaking in terms of this earthen vessel, we were without formation. We were chaotic, void and empty of knowledge and wisdom, void of understanding unlearned and ignorant. We were sinners and we needed a savior.

Darkness was upon the face of the deep.
(Genesis 1:2b)

Our countenance means a person's face or facial expressions. Our attitude means a natural ability to do something. It wasn't framed or fashioned for suitability or fitness, it was out of shape. A natural tendency couldn't do things normally. We were tore up from the floor up. We were walking in darkness before we gave Jesus our lives. We were void and empty of His wisdom, knowledge, and understanding. But God sent his Only Begotten Son that whosoever believeth on him should not perish but have everlasting life.

How was this world created, formed, framed, or fashioned? God's faith, His Word.

> *But without faith it is impossible to please him.*
> *(Hebrews 11:6)*

Look what happens when you don't operate by faith. It's like a gun with no ammunition, no power, useless. It's like an air condition without Freon. Without Jesus your life is fruitless. It's like you start a task but you never finish it. It's thrown on the back burner. There are books inside of you that have never been revealed, songs that has never been sung or written. We need the connection of the True Vine.

> *And the Spirit of God moved upon the face of the waters or the deep.*
> *(Genesis 1:2)*

What happens when you do have faith? We can speak to mountains and they have to move!

For he that cometh to God must believe that He is, and that He is a rewarder or revealer

of them that diligently seek him.
(Hebrews 11:6)

There is a reward when you diligently earnestly seek Him.

I always use my A S K code.

Ask Seek Knock- Jesus says if I ask I shall receive. If I seek I shall find. If I knock the door shall be opened. (Matthew 7: 7-8)

When this happens, your faith gets stronger and stronger.

Chapter 17
Faith in God Never Fails

I always asked questions because I needed to know answers. For some reason people feel as though they can't ask God, their Father, what they want to know. I don't have a problem with asking my Daddy about anything. Once I got to know who my real Father was, I was delighted to be able to talk to Him. That's how it should be with all of God's children. There ain't nothing I can't talk to my Daddy about because I know He loves me and He has my best interest in mind. So Daddy how did You do all this?

He answers, by faith my daughter. (Hebrews 11:3)

By faith, by believing God, we know that the world and the stars, in fact, all things were made or framed at God's command; and that they were all made from things that can't be seen. God causes the invisible (faith) to become the visible. Your requests your prayers to come to pass.
(Hebrews 11:1-2)

What is faith? It is the confident assurance that something we want is going to happen. It is the certainty that what we hope for is waiting for us, even though we cannot see it up ahead.

Men of God in days of old were famous for their faith. How? By an invisible God who became visible through His Word, Jesus Christ, to us. God framed His change. Whenever God's spirit moves upon or within He speaks and things change and appear. God's imagination is taking on formation now. Being manifested!

What did God do to bring forth light? When the breath of God's Word is breathed or spoken into a soul light and life comes forth.

How do we get this Faith? It comes by hearing and hearing by the Word of God. (Romans 10:17)

Next, God starts to speak what he wants to come to pass.

> *And God said, Let there be light:*
> *and there was light.*
> (Genesis 1:3)

> *He calleth those things which*
> *be not as though they were.*
> (Romans 4:17)

Once faith spoke out then the light was manifested.

> *And God saw the light, that it was good.*
> (Genesis 1:4)

He spoke over what he desired to come to pass. Then what was invisible became visible then he put his stamp of approval on it and called it is good!

> *...and God divided the light*
> *from the darkness.*
> (Genesis 1:4b)

God knows how to separate that which is causing darkness and trouble in your life. Once darkness is moved from your life, He replaces it with light, illumination, and understanding. This is what I call an umbrella to start the process of your faithful and faith filled life of provision and protection from the rains the storms of life. Next, He said what He wanted to happened. He made a sky and a heaven.

And God said, let there be a firmament in the midst of the waters, and let it divide the waters from the waters. And God made the firmament, and divided the waters which were under the firmament from the waters which were above the firmament: and it was so.
(Genesis 1: 6-7)

The sky and the heavens, were then created. Then he named the seas, oceans, rivers, and lakes. He then called the firmament heaven on the second day. The third day He said for the waters under the heaven to be gathered together unto one place, and let the dry land appear that was earth.

Notice how He orchestrated and organized this earth for His purpose and plan for our life. One of the definitions for orchestrated is to arrange or direct the elements of (a situation) to produce a desired effect, especially surreptitiously.

Interesting God knew that everyone would not approve of the way He had planned and orchestrated this world, so He had to frame the change, so that no one else could change His frame.

The word surreptitiously means to keep secret, especially because it would not be approved of. That's amazing for us who are saved. God's Word says, the secret things belong to the Lord our God but those things which are revealed, belong unto us and our children forever, that we may do all the words of this Law or Word. (Deuteronomy 29:29) Everything He had planned was for our good and it was very good He did it one day at a time.

There is an enemy out there and he is doing a darn devilish job. He wants to keep your mind focus off of everything good and the very good life God has created for all of the saints to have in this life and the life to come. He is subtle and deceptive. That's why Jesus tells us to watch as well as pray. The devil's objective is to keep your eyes, ears, and mind focus on the knowledge the media of good and evil instead of focusing on the perfect will or Word that God has given you from the beginning. When you do that then you repeat whatever the media or whoever says and you run with it and you keep repeating it. Don't keep nursing and rehearsing bad news. Learn this lesson today, speak what God says only.

We're not going to be ignorant of the devil's devices. Keep your mind focus on good things. (Philippians 4:8)Switch the channel of your mind to who you were created to be, healthy, wealthy and wise.

The things that are happening should be no surprise to us. All you see now from this point on is, it is written.

Chapter 18
Don't Play Around, Watch as Well as Pray

You may as well know this too, Timothy, that in the last days it is going to be very difficult to be a Christian. For people will love only themselves and their money; they will be proud and boastful, sneering at God, disobedient to their parents, ungrateful to them, and thoroughly bad. They will be hardheaded and never give in to others; they will be constant liars and troublemakers and will think nothing of immorality. They will be rough and cruel, and sneer at those who try to be good. They will betray their friends; they will be hotheaded, puffed up with pride, and prefer good times to worshiping God. They will go to church, yes, but they won't really believe anything they hear. Don't be taken in by people like that. They are the kind who craftily sneak into other people's homes and make friendships with silly, sin-burdened women and teach them their new doctrines.

> *Women of that kind are forever following new teachers,*
> *but they never understand the truth.*
> (2 Timothy 3: 1-7)

But in the same chapter, when all this trouble came upon him and the afflictions of all those who despised the truth of God's word, he said the Lord delivered him out of them all.

Always remember there is a different outcome for all those who believe. Your going through something is always going to something greater and better for the purpose of the Kingdom of God.

> *You know how many troubles I have had as a result of my preaching the Good News. You know about all that was done to me while I was visiting in Antioch, Iconium, and Lystra, but the Lord delivered me.*
> (2 Timothy 3:11)

So if the Lord can deliver him, surely He can deliver you and I.

Frame your world with the words you want it to be. Then conquer, defeat, and speak to any mountain be thou removed in Jesus name. Frame it and claim it. The Word is final authority.

Janice Randolph Founder/Pastor of Redeemed to Dominate Church of the Living God

P.O. Box 321302
Flint, Michigan 48532
Phone # 810-241-6081
Email- janran54@comcast.net
Face Book Page- Janice Graham-Randolph
Twitter -JaniceRandolph@jancan54

Entrepreneur

Website: www.gogf.net or
Go Girlfriend Shine for Jesus Inc.

Psalmist/Speaker

Host and Producer of Stand Step up and Stretch Out For Jesus on Comcast Cable Television Channel 17
Flint, Michigan
Mondays 9:30 PM, Wednesday 7:00 AM
Fridays 8:30 PM

Southfield, Michigan Comcast Cable Television 6:00 PM

Author Bio

On June 5, 1954 in Lake Wales, Florida, Mary Hughes and Alonzo Graham became the parents of Janice Randolph. She was reared by her grandparents, Earl and Mint Graham. She spent most of her child years in Ft Meade, Florida. While there, she attended Ft Meade High School. She later graduated from Crenshaw High School in Los Angeles, California-1972. As an undergraduate student, she attended Southland College of Medical and Dental careers in Los Angeles California. She graduated where she obtained her degree as a Dental Assistant. She has served in the Dental industry for 45 yrs.

Now launching into a deeper part of her field, she utilizes the knowledge and the gift of character building she has gained over the years. She's been in dentistry using the gift to work in mouths, with her hands, now she uses her gift to show how to utilize the very thing she has helped others with... to look beautiful cosmetically for outer appearance, to feel good about themselves and that is your mouth. Janice has worked in the mouth for all these years, now she has moved on to what she really loves most and that is to bless others by speaking and giving good godly principles and changing lives.

The new launch is to be the best author, consultant, counselor, booster, encourager, minister/ Pastor and constructive helper. Her desire is to see others become the best they can be and love doing what they do. She knows this does not mean without stress, and free from every problem, but having solutions to the problems that arise in life, business or church.

Janice is the Founder of Go Girlfriend Shine For Jesus Inc. She is also excited about being the Pastor of Redeemed to Dominate Church of The Living God. The Church is Non-Denominational and is a multicultural body of believers of the true Church of our Lord and savior Jesus Christ. She caters to the community and ministers to God's people all over the world. She counsels and teaches people who have been battered and oppressed from broken and problem marriages, and children with all types of issues.

Janice is also a Minister of music and a Psalmist. She has traveled to various parts of the nation and the world ministering in praise and worship and ministering the Word of God. She is a supporter and pastor of several churches in Kenya, Africa. She also helps young ladies to pursue their God given talents in sending them to college so they will realize they were created to prosper and be in health not poverty as some believe in their country. This is done by the help of several supporters.

Janice has three Christian Television programs on Comcast Community channel 17. On every Monday at 9:30pm in Flint, Michigan, Wednesday 7:00 am, the other every Sunday at 6:00pm in Southfield, Michigan.

Janice has three wonderful children, Kenyata Wesley, Lasheca Hairston and Calvin Randolph Jr. She has two beautiful daughter-in-laws, Keisha Wesley, Maria Randolph and a wonderful son-in-law Kareem Hairston. She also has precious grandchildren and twin great grands.

Remember, "All things are possible with God, to those who believe on Him."

Life can be like a Log Ride at Cedar Point sometimes

Feel good going up, exciting, fun, enjoyable

But when you're coming down,
It's scarey, you're going all around
You're screaming, hollering, saying
"Let Me Off This Thing!

But then after all the screaming, yelling & saying Let Me Off This Thing, you're ready to go back and stand in that long line and do it again

Life is full of ups and downs just keep holding on and remember with God all things are possible to those who believeand never give up or give in.

Log in at gogf.net & be Blessed

DVD's and CD's Available for Purchase:

To Order DVD's or CD's Please:

Visit: www.gogf.net

or call

(810) 241-6081

To Order More Copies of this Book Please:

Visit: www.gogf.net

or call

(810) 241-6081

www.ingramcontent.com/pod-product-compliance
Lightning Source LLC
Chambersburg PA
CBHW050654160426
43194CB00010B/1938